Table of Contents

EDCON PUBLISHING

www.edconpublishing.com

Surprise Pies

Mr. Butternut turned out the fire under the big oven in his bakery. "I've made my last pie," he announced.

"Oh, dear," sighed Mrs. Butternut. "They are such excellent pies. And cheap, too!"

"Excellent!" shouted Mr. Butternut. "Of course they're excellent. I make the very best pies in the whole wide world!"

"We know you do," said Mrs. Butternut. "But nobody else tastes your pies any more. Hardly anyone knows how good they are. It's a shame!"

It was all very true.

The people of the Frosting Village bought pies from Mr. Whistletoe, whose prices were high. He was the favorite baker of the rich Mr. Stump. Where Mr. Stump shopped, all the other village men and their wives shopped, too. So poor Mr. Butternut did not have any customers left.

All of a sudden Mr. Butternut said, "I wish our pies were magic!"

"Dear me!" exclaimed his wife. "Don't wish that!"

"But just imagine!" said Mr. Butternut. "If our

pies were magic, we could sell them. Let's wish them to be magic."

"Oh, dear!" cried Mrs. Butternut faintly. But she closed her eyes and began to wish.

Mr. Butternut was already wishing.

Soon he opened his eyes and said, "Now! Let's find out if our wishing worked. Hand me a black-berry pie."

Mrs. Butternut brought the pie, and her husband drew a sharp knife across it.

As soon as he cut the pie, out flew three red-headed woodpeckers!

For a minute the baker was too amazed to say a word.

When he was able to speak, he whispered hoarsely, "P-P-Please bring me another pie."

Mrs. Butternut brought over a peach pie.

Mr. Butternut sliced through it.

Out sprang three white mice.

Mr. Butternut was getting more and more excited.

"Our pies are magic!" he shouted. "Our pies are full of magic surprises!"

That very afternoon the baker put up a big sign outside his shop. The sign said,

TRY OUR SURPRISE PIES.

CUT THEM AND SEE WHAT JUMPS OUT!

The sign began to bring in customers.

Mrs. Cartwheel was the first one to buy a surprise pie. When she cut into it, she screamed with pleasure.

Out jumped a tiny kitten.

Soon Mrs. Penny dashed in and got a pie. As she cut it, out popped a cunning monkey. A pet monkey was exactly what Mrs. Penny had always wanted.

Young Molly Twinkle bought the next pie and cut into it eagerly. To her delight, out popped a doll in a pink silk dress.

Old Mrs. Potter was the next customer. When she cut her pie, she saw a whistling teakettle.

"It's just what I've always needed!" she exclaimed.

It was not long before the rich Mr. Stump heard about the amazing pies. He sent one of his servants to the shop at once.

"Baker!" the servant cried. "Mr. Stump wants the biggest and best apple pie you can make."

Mr. Butternut squirmed with delight.

"Yes, sir!" he cried. "I'll bake a fresh pie just for Mr. Stump. It'll be the most surprising pie of all."

The baker worked carefully until he had made a twenty-inch pie. It was juicy and golden brown. It had a delicious smell.

"Here it is," the proud baker said to the servant. "Here is a huge magic pie for Mr. Stump."

The happy Mr. Butternut began to dance and whirl around the shop.

"We'll be rich," the baker shouted. "Mr. Stump will surely like our big surprise pie! He'll like it so much that he'll buy a lot of pies. Then everyone else will buy them."

"Yes," said Mrs. Butternut unhappily. "But suppose that Mr. Stump cuts into the pie, and suppose that something jumps out which he doesn't like. Just imagine that!"

Mr. Butternut stopped dancing. He looked shocked and scared for an instant. Then he said, "Just imagine a tiger jumping out!"

"How awful!" cried Mrs. Butternut. "Mr. Stump would be terribly frightened. He'd have us locked up. Oh, if only we hadn't wished our pies to be magic!"

"Well, then," said Mr. Butternut quickly. "Let's wish them not to be magic!"

So they wished and wished and wished. They were still wishing when Mr. Stump's servant came running into the bakery.

"Follow me!" he ordered.

Pale with fright, Mr. and Mrs. Butternut soon were standing before the rich man.

"See here," shouted Mr. Stump in a loud voice. "I cut into this pie, but no surprise jumped out."

"Oh, dear," gasped Mrs. Butternut.

"But," said Mr. Stump in a louder tone, "I had a nice surprise anyway."

"You did?" asked Mr. Butternut timidly.

"Yes, indeed," replied Mr. Stump. "Even though no surprise jumped out of the pie, it tasted good. Simply delicious!"

Mr. Stump gobbled another piece.

"From now on," he said, "you shall bake me a pie for every meal!"

After that, Mr. Butternut sold all the pies he could bake. Not magic ones! Just real, delicious pies that everyone loved to eat.

Snow White and Rose Red

There was once a poor widow who lived in a little cottage at the edge of a forest. In front of the cottage bloomed two rose-trees, one with red flowers and one with white. The widow had two daughters, so pretty and sweet that she named them after the rose-trees, Rose-Red and Snow-White.

Snow-White was quiet and gentle in all her ways. Rose-Red was merrier. She was likely to be off chasing butterflies while Snow-White was helping her mother in the house.

But the two girls loved their mother and loved each other dearly. And they were so kind and good that no animal in all the forest would harm them.

One cold winter evening, while the kettle sang on the hearth and the mother was reading a story to the girls, there came a knock at the door.

"Open the door, Rose-Red!" the mother cried. "Perhaps, this bitter night, some traveler has lost his way."

So Rose-Red unlached the door. But there instead of a poor traveler, stood a great black bear! Rose-Red was frightened. And she would've shut the door again, but the bear called out to her in a man's voice.

"Do not be afraid," said the bear. "I'll do you no harm. But I am half-frozen, and beg that I may warm myself at your fire."

"Poor bear!" said the mother. "Come lie beside the hearth. Only take care not to get a spark on your shaggy coat."

"My fur is full of snow." Said the bear. "Perhaps your daughters would bring brooms and sweep it off before I come in."

So Snow-White and Rose-Red got their brooms and swept the bear. Then he lay down before the fire. In a little while the girls forgot completely to be afraid of him. He was such a gentle, kind bear! They romped with him and pulled his fur and played so many tricks that more than once he called out:

Children dear, leave me my life,
Or else you'll never be called wife.

When bedtime came, the mother said, "You may stay here and sleep, if you like." So the bear slept before the hearth, and the children let him out in the morning. Every evening after that, all winter long, the bear came trotting to the cottage, and the door was never barred until he came.

But, with the spring, the woods turned green. The birds began to return. One morning, when Snow-White came to let the bear out, he seemed quite sad.

"Dear Snow-White," he said sighing, "I must say goodbye for a while."

"Alas dear bear," said Snow-White, "where are you going?"

"I must stay in the forest to guard my treasures," he answered. "In the winter the evil dwarfs are kept in their holes by the snow and the ice. But in the summer the dwarfs go everywhere, and they are great thieves."

So Snow-White opened the door for her friend. But she opened it slowly and sadly. As the bear pushed through, he tore his shaggy coat. Snow-White was not sure, but for a moment she thought she saw a golden gleam under the fur.

Some time afterwards, Rose-Red and Snow-White went into the forest to gather sticks for the fire.

"What is that," Rose-Red asked, "Bobbing up and down on the lawn?"

The girls went near to see. There was a dwarf with a snowy white beard a yard long! His beard was caught in the crack in the log, and the little man was hopping around trying to pull himself free.

He glared at the girls with his little red eyes. "Don't just stand there, you great stupid girls!" he snapped. "Help me get loose."

"How did you happen to get caught here?" Rose-Red asked, as she helped to pull.

"Of all the foolish questions!" panted the dwarf. "An idiot could see that as I was splitting this log for firewood, the wedge slipped and the log closed up again."

But no matter how they pulled, the children could not get the little man's beard free.

"Well," said Snow-White, "there is only one thing to do." And taking her scissors out of her pocket she cut off the end of the dwarf's beard.

The little fellow was not a bit grateful. "Plague take you!" he screamed. "You have spoiled my beautiful beard. May bad luck follow you!" And he jumped up, seized a sack of gold which lay hidden in the roots of the tree, and marched off.

A few days later Snow-White and Rose-Red

went fishing. As they drew near the pond, they heard a shrill little voice and saw something jumping up and down. It was the dwarf again.

"Help me, you!" he screamed when he saw them. "This brute of a fish is pulling me into the water!"

And so it was. Somehow the dwarf's beard and the fishing line had got tangled up together, just as a large fish came along. The girls were soon able to rescue the little man from the fish. But getting the fishing line untangled from his beard was a harder matter. Again, Snow-White slipped out her scissors. She cut two more little pieces off his beard.

"Donkey!" screamed the little man. "May the crows peck you for ruining my beautiful beard!" He took up a bag of pearls which lay nearby in the rushes, and slipped away.

Not very many days later the girls were on their way to town, to buy needles and thread and ribbon for their mother. Their road lay across an open place strewn with large rocks. Above the rocks a bird was circling. As they watched it, they saw it dive and heard a scream. Running up, they found that the bird had seized their old acquaintance the dwarf, and was trying to carry him off.

The girls laid hold of the dwarf and soon frightened the bird away. They were used to the little man, and were not surprised when he said, "Great, clumsy things! Why did you have to tear my coat?" And picking up a bag of precious stones, he disappeared.

On their way back from town, the girls passed the same place. They came upon the dwarf again. He had emptied his bag of stones onto a large, flat rock, and was letting them slip through his fingers. With the sun shining through them, the stones were so beautiful that the girls stopped to admire them.

The dwarf saw them watching him. He jumped up in a fury. "So you want to steal my stones!" he yelled. "Get away, or I will do you an injury." And he picked up a large stone to throw at them.

Just at this moment a big black bear rushed out of the forest near by. The dwarf saw him and tried to run, but he was not fast enough.

"Spare me, dear bear!" begged the dwarf. "Eat up those stupid girls instead. They'll make a much better meal than poor little me."

The bear only growled and gave the dwarf one

blow with his big paw. And that was the end of the dwarf.

Rose-Red and Snow-White were running away in fright, when a voice they knew called after them "Do not run, children. It is I."

And there was their own friend the bear. As he came up to them, suddenly his rough coat fell off. A handsome young man dressed in gold stood there!

"I am a king's son," he said. "This wicked dwarf stole all my treasures, and turned me into a bear. Only his death would set me free. But until today I could never catch him.

So they all went home rejoicing. In time Snow-White married the prince and Rose-Red married his brother. And they took their mother to the palace to live with them. In front of the palace, for years and years, the red and white rose-trees bloomed all summer long.

The Emperor's New Clothes

Long, long ago there was an Emperor who was more interested in clothes than anything else in the world. He had a special outfit for every day of the week, and every hour of the day.

One day two rogues came to town, pretending they were expert weavers and tailors. The two men set up a loom and spread the news that they wove the finest of cloth, in the most beautiful designs and colors. But, said they, only a really wise man could see it, for to stupid, dull or foolish people it was completely invisible.

The Emperor said he must have a suit of this marvelous cloth. So he immediately sent for these men and ordered them to make him a royal costume. He gave them a bag of gold and told them to spare no expense.

The two rogues stuffed their purses and made a great show of working on the empty looms at all hours of the night and day. Two weeks went by, then the Emperor, who could hardly wait to try on his wonderful new clothes, sent his trusted minister to see how the work was going.

When the minister arrived at the shop he saw the two rogues hard at work, going through all the motions of weaving. He could see no cloth, but the two men described the lovely colors and delicate designs in such glowing words that the minister thought, I must be the greatest fool in the kingdom, for I can see nothing! Yet if I tell the Emperor that the looms are bare, he will think I am stupid and discharge me. I had better repeat to him the words of the weavers. So he went back to the Emperor and praised the rich color and delicate patterns.

A week later, when the cloth was still not finished, the Emperor sent another trusted official to examine the weavers' work. The official could see nothing on the loom either, because of course there was nothing there to see. But he did not want to be thought a fool, so he too, praised the cloth, telling the Emperor that its gorgeous design would be sure to dazzle all who beheld it.

The Emperor was growing so impatient, that he decided to see for himself. With a party of courtiers he arrived at the shop of the two rogues who were weaving at the empty loom.

"Did Your Majesty ever behold such gorgeous

material?" asked the one. "Just feel the quality!" said the other. Bewildered, the Emperor looked at his courtiers, but they were all smiling, exclaiming, "Exquisite!" "Oh, Perfect!" "Magnificent!" The Emperor said to himself, "No one must know how stupid I am." And he, too, began to praise the cloth that wasn't there.

Soon the great Procession of the Year was to take place, and the two rogues promised the Emperor that his new suit would be ready for the occasion. Each of the men was given a knight's medal to hang in his buttonhole and with it the title of "Gentleman in Weaving."

The night before the Procession, the two rogues worked late into the night making the royal costume. They lit all the candles in the shop so that everyone could see they were hard at work. They snipped the empty air with scissors, they sewed with threadless needles, and at last they pulled out the long bastings, stood up, and shook out the beautiful clothes that were not there.

In the morning the Emperor came to try on the suit. He stood straight and still while he let them take away his clothes and put on the imaginary new ones. "Light as a spider's web," said the one, going through the motions of slipping on the coat. "What superb color!" said the other, throwing the invisible mantle over the Emperor's shoulder. And the attending courtiers echoed, "Oh, Superb! Superb!"

So the Emperor walked proudly under the royal canopy in the Procession. He was sure that his new clothes made him look magnificent, although he could not see them.

He bowed graciously to the left and right, as the people cried, "How splendid are the Emperor's new clothes! How beautifully they fit! Such color, such rare and costly cloth!"

Then all at once a little child cried, "But he hasn't got anything on!" And though his mother hushed him quickly, the Emperor had heard. Perhaps the child was right! The thought made his flesh creep but he knew that being the Emperor, he must lead the Procession through to the end. So he squared his shoulders and held his head high while the lords in waiting followed, bearing the train that wasn't there at all!

The Three Bears

Once upon a time, there were Three Bears who lived together in a house of their own in a deep green woods. One of them was a small wee Bear, and one was a middle-sized Bear, and the other was a great big Bear. Each had a bowl for his porridge; a little bowl for the small wee Bear, a middle-sized bowl for the middle-sized Bear, and a large bowl for the great big Bear. And each had a chair to sit in; a small wee chair for the small wee Bear, a middle-sized chair for the middle-sized Bear, and a great big chair for the great big Bear. And each had a bed to sleep in; a small wee bed for the small wee Bear, a middle-sized bed for the middle-sized Bear, and a great big bed for the great big Bear.

One day, after they had cooked the porridge for their breakfast and poured it into their porridge bowls, they walked out into the woods to wait for the porridge to cool. When they were out walking, a little golden-haired girl, called Goldilocks, came to the house. She could not have been a well-behaved little girl for she peeped in at the keyhole; then, seeing no one in the house, she lifted the latch. The door was not fastened because the Bears were good Bears who never harmed anyone and never suspected that anyone would talk into their house without an invitation. But Goldilocks opened the door and walked into the house. She was well-pleased when she saw the three bowls of porridge on the table. Now if she had been polite little girl she would have waited until the Three Bears came home, and then perhaps they would have asked her to stay for breakfast, for they were good Bears. But the porridge looked very delicious, so Goldilocks did not wait.

First she tasted the porridge of the great big Bear, but it was too hot for her. Then she tasted the porridge of the middle-sized Bear, but that was too cold. And then she tasted the porridge of the small wee Bear, and that was just right. So she ate it all up!

Then Goldilocks sat down in the chair of the great big Bear, but it was too hard and uncomfort-able. Next she sat down in the chair of the middle-sized Bear, but that was too soft. Then she sat down in the chair of the small wee Bear and that was just right. She sat there until suddenly the bottom of the chair fell out, and down she went plump upon the floor!

Then Goldilocks went upstairs into the bedroom where the Three Bears slept. First she lay down upon the bed of the great big Bear, but it was too hard and uncomfortable for her. Next she lay down upon the bed of the middle-sized Bear, but it was too soft. Then she lay upon the bed of the small wee Bear, and it was just right. So she covered herself up with the quilts and lay there and fell fast asleep.

By this time the Three Bears thought their porridge was cool enough for them to eat; so they went home to breakfast. Goldilocks had left the spoon of the great big Bear standing in his porridge bow.

"SOMEBODY HAS BEEN EATING MY PORRIDGE!" said the great big Bear in his great big, rough, gruff voice.

And when the middle-sized Bear looked at hers, she saw a spoon was in her bowl too.

"SOMEBODY'S BEEN EATING MY PORRIDGE!" said the middle-sized Bear in her middle-sized voice.

Then the small wee Bear looked at his bowl and there, too, was a spoon in it, but the bowl was empty.

"SOMEBODY HAS BEEN EATING MY
PORRIDGE AND IT'S ALL GONE!"
said the small wee Bear in his little, small, wee
voice.

Upon seeing this, the Three Bears knew some-
one had entered their house and eaten up the small
wee Bear's porridge. So they began to look about
them.

Now Goldilocks had not put the hard cushion
straight in the chair of the great big Bear.

"SOMEBODY'S BEEN SITTING IN MY
CHAIR!" said the great big Bear in his great big,
rough, gruff voice.

Goldilocks had crushed down the soft cushions
lying in the chair of the middle-sized Bear.

"SOMEBODY'S BEEN SITTING IN MY
CHAIR!" said the middle-sized Bear in her middle-
sized voice.

And you know what Goldilocks had done to the
third chair.

"SOMEBODY HAS BEEN SITTING IN MY
CHAIR AND HAS SAT THE BOTTOM OUT OF
IT!"

Said the small wee Bear in his little, small, wee voice.

Then the Three Bears certainly were disturbed and knew they must make a further search. So they went into their bedroom.

Now Goldilocks had pulled the pillow of the great big Bear out of its place.

"SOMEBODY'S BEEN LYING IN MY BED!" said the great big Bear in his great big, rough, gruff voice.

And Goldilocks had pulled the quilts out of place on the middle-sized Bear's bed.

"SOMEBODY'S BEEN LYING IN MY BED!" said the middle-sized Bear in her middle-sized voice.

And when the small wee Bear came to look at his bed, he saw the pillow in its place, and resting upon the pillow was little golden-haired Goldilock's head.

"SOMEBODY HAS BEEN LYING IN
MY BED-AND HERE SHE IS!"
Said the small wee Bear in his little, small, wee voice.

Goldilocks had heard in her sleep the great,

big, rough gruff voice of the great big Bear, and the middle-sized voice of the middle-sized Bear but she thought she was dreaming. However, when she heard the little, small, wee voice of the small wee Bear, it was so sharp and so shrill that it awakened her at once.

Up she started; and when she discovered the Three Bears standing on one side of the bed, she tumbled out the other side and ran to the window. The window was open. So Goldilocks jumped out and ran home as fast as she could. Never again did the Three Bears see anything of the little golden-haired Goldilocks.

The Mixed-Up Family

Once there was a very odd family named Floogle. There were Mr. and Mrs. Floogle and their children, Flower and Amos. There was also their dog, Sniffy.

The Floogles were nice people. But they were always getting excited and mixed up.

One day a picture-taking man came a long. He was a very old man, and his camera was heavy. When he saw the Floogles working in the yard, he called to them.

"Excuse me," he said. "Could I have a drink of water?"

Mrs. Floogle said, "Water? Come into my kitchen and have a glass of cold milk."

Soon everyone was scurrying all about. Mrs. Floogle filled a glass with cold milk. Amos cut some ham for a sandwich. Flower got a plate full of cookies. Mr. Floogle cut some cheese. Sniffy sat up and begged.

When the old man had finished his tasty lunch, he said, "Thank you. Now I'll pay you back for your kindness. I'll take a picture of you."

Immediately the Floogles became excited. They chattered noisily as they got ready.

Finally they all quieted down, and the man told them where to stand for the picture. He put Sniffy right in front, since he was the smallest.

Then the man stepped behind his camera and pulled a black cloth over his head. He was ready to take the picture.

But Mr. Floogle said, "This won't do! Flower should be in front so that everyone will notice how nice her curls look."

Flower moved in front beside Sniffy, and the man got ready to snap the camera.

But Mrs. Floogle said, "Oh, this won't do. Amos must be in front, too. Everyone will want to see how straight his new front teeth are."

So Amos stood in front with Flower, and Sniffy sat between them.

Again the old man got ready to take the picture.

But Flower said, "Stop! This won't do. Mother must stand in front. Everyone will want to see her lovely new dress!"

By this time the old man had grown quite warm and tired. He wiped his face with his handkerchief and said, "I'll rest while you make up your minds. When you decide where you'll stand in the picture call me."

With that, he sat down in a soft chair and fell sound asleep.

At last the family made up their minds.

"Now!" said Mr. Floogle. "Everybody get in front. Then we'll each be seen clearly."

"Look!" said Mrs. Floogle. "The old man is asleep. It seems too bad to call him."

"Let's not wake him," said Amos. "I can take the picture myself by squeezing the little black ball on that cord. The cord is long enough for me to be in the picture and still squeeze the black ball."

First Amos peeked under the cloth to see how the picture would look.

"Oh, my goodness!" he shouted. "This is terrible! You are upside down."

Mr. Floogle took a peek.

"You are indeed upside down!" he cried.

"That is a shame!" cried Mrs. Floogle. "The old man was trying to be nice to us. If his camera takes pictures upside down, we must do something about it."

The family thought and thought.

Suddenly they laughed and clapped their hands. They all had the same idea.

"We want our picture right side up," said Amos. "So here's what we must do. We'll all have to..."

"Of course," said Mrs. Floogle eagerly. "Lets get in our places."

"How about Sniffy?" asked Flower.

"I'm afraid it's impossible for Sniffy to be in this picture," said Mr. Floogle.

Everybody got ready again.

Just before Amos took his place in the picture, he peeked under the black cloth.

"Now you look all right," he said happily. "Everybody keep perfectly quiet and smile."

"One, two, three!" said Mr. Floogle.

Everybody took a deep breath and smiled.

Amos squeezed the little black ball.

"There! It's done," he said. "The nice gentleman can go on sleeping."

The sun had already set when the old man woke up from his nap. He rubbed his eyes and said, "Oh, I must take the picture!"

Then the Floogles told him that they had taken the picture themselves.

"Well!" the man exclaimed in surprise. "Now I have work to do. I'll finish the picture in a few minutes."

Taking a piece of glass from his camera, he went to the kitchen.

When he finished the picture, he was so amazed that he called to the family.

"Look here!" he said. "Why did you take the picture standing like this?"

"Oh!" said Mr. Floogle. "That's the only way we looked right in the camera."

The old man burst into laughter.

"You see," he explained, "people always look upside down in a camera like mine. But the picture comes out with the people right side up. Well, I'll take another picture."

All the Floogles liked the picture the way it was. Their friends liked it, too.

"Hold the picture up," they would say to each other. "Hold it up so that the family is right side up, and all the furniture hangs front the ceiling."

"Now hold it so that the furniture stands on the floor, and the people stand upside down on their heads. Oh, it's all so very mixed up!"

And it was. The Floogles were so mixed up that all their friends felt mixed up, too.

A Valentine Story

Long, ago there lived in a faraway country two boys. These boys were just like boys today because they liked to play. But the people who lived near didn't like to hear the noise they made when they were having their good times.

Once when they were playing a new game, a messenger left them a note which said,

"You will not be allowed to play on the street any more. If you do, you will be punished."

This made the two boys unhappy.

Then Benedict, the older boy, told Julius that they would take the note to their friend Valentine, an old man who lived in a house with a large garden. Valentine loved children and was always kind to them. When he read the note, he smiled and said,

"You may come into my garden and play. I am sure no one will stop you there."

Every day the boys walked quietly down the street. But the minute they were inside the garden wall they could run and shout as much as they pleased.

One day the boys went to the garden and found

the gate locked. No one answered when they knocked. They waited and waited. Then they went home and tried to be quiet, but it was very hard.

The boys had not heard about Valentine. They did not know that the King had sent him to prison for the rest of his life. Valentine was wondering how he could send the boys the key to the garden gate. At last he thought of a plan.

One day the boys were looking out the window. They were unhappy because they could not run and play. And suddenly a white pigeon flew down to the window sill. Around the pigeon's leg a key and a note were tied. Benedict held the pigeon gently while Julius untied the key and the note.

The note read,

"This key will open the garden gate for two boys I love."

Then the boys were happy because they knew that Valentine remembered them.

As the boys grew older, they learned that Valentine had sent messages to all his friends. This is why people send messages of love on Valentine's birthday. This is why the fourteenth of February is called Saint Valentine's Day.